The Dream Dictionary

A Guide to Understanding and Interpreting Your Dreams

Lauren Lingard

Table of Content

Introduction 1

Chapter One: Why We Dream 3

Chapter Two: Record Your Dreams 5

Chapter Three: What Do Your Dreams Mean? 7

Chapter Four: Recurring Dreams, Deja Vu, & Lucid Dreaming 51

Final Words 54

Introduction

Never, in the history of man, have dreams not been questioned or pondered. As humans, we ask time and again what they mean and where they come from. Whether over centuries, country lines, or languages, humankind has come to determine that dreams mean things, and what they mean can either be a universal concept, or simply just what they mean for us. In fact, it was the ancient Babylonians who first began recording their dreams, on stone tablets no less, for the purpose of interpreting them.

From the beginnings of society to the modern age, we look within to find answers to life's most arduous questions, oftentimes the answers being already within us. Dreams have been a bandage and salve for some of these aching wonders. However bizarre, it is dreams that sometimes give us the best advice, clues, or ideas. Stephanie Meyer, after all, got the idea for her bestselling saga, *Twilight*, from a dream.

With the evolution of scientific inquiry, we know now that most dreams happen during REM sleep, when the brain is most active during the sleep cycle. Dreams during this period of time are rich and vibrant. We tend to remember these most graphically and in the most detail. While some experts claim that dreaming could be reduced down to the brain's coping mechanism to deal with the daily stressors of life, others suggest that there is another force at play. Does this mean that the human brain is much more creative and imaginative than previously thought? What else is the brain capable of during sleep and what more can we discover about how we dream?

The series of images that our brain conjures come together, like a woven rug, to form a narrative or what we call a dream. A dream is nothing more than a quick succession of pictures put together from our brain, but they are placed together so quickly, it often feels as if we are watching a movie. While most people have between three and five dreams a night, most of those are quickly and easily forgotten. Some people do not even remember having dreams most nights. Although disappointing, it is important to remember that the dreams still happen, and most likely for a reason.

Through careful analysis and consideration, *The Dream Dictionary* seeks to answer questions about dreaming and offer perspective of what the little pieces of our dream puzzles mean. In these pages, maybe you, too, will find the salve or bandage your dream is trying to be for you.

Chapter One: Why We Dream

A hotly debated topic, why we dream, remains a question we have yet to find many answers to. Many theories circulate, but there is a distinct lack of definitive answers as to why the brain chooses to give us these visual interpretations. What we know from recent studies is that the brain operates between a certain range of hertz during the sleep process that produces theta waves. This period of sleep is when most of the dreaming occurs. Evidence from a study on a group of twenty in the United Kingdom's Swansea University, suggests that dreaming could be a coping mechanism to help with the emotional processing of difficult or stressful events.

Furthermore, one of the reasons that we sleep could be to help solve our problems and to use old memories before they are forgotten. It is no secret that the brain has a myriad of complex processes to deal with trauma, pain, and discomfort, so it is not a stretch to say that dreaming is an addition to these capabilities.

For a long time, theories have stated that dreams mean nothing and have just evolved from a process that the human body no longer uses. Others argue that dreams are a universal connection between humankind and the world we reside in, drawing upon the natural energy in the world to give us messages. This is harder to prove, of course, but it is a commonly held belief.

Similarly, theologians attest that Biblical resources mention that God gives dreams. Gods and Goddesses of Dreams are also littered across the pantheons of the ancient world. Morpheus, for example, is the Greco-Roman God of Dreams and Sleep.

What some experts have found, however, is that the brain simply acts differently during these cycles of sleep and wakefulness. Numerous studies have been done to show the effect of dreaming on mental, physical, and emotional health. Those who were woken before going into REM sleep, and thus did not dream, struggled more with mental health.

Regardless of the science of why we dream, it cannot be argued that the benefits of dreaming are understated. Dreams manifest ideas, bring new perspectives, and offer refreshing breaks from the stressors in daily life.

Chapter Two: Record Your Dreams

The earliest known recording of dreams goes back to 3100 BCE from the Ancient Babylonians, who had already enveloped the idea of writing down and interpreting dreams on stone tablets. The same culture who fathered the famous hanging gardens, one of the Ancient Seven Wonders of The World, was founded in what was called Mesopotamia, or the Cradle of Civilization. Even the most sophisticated of humanity's ancestors had an interest in recording dreams.

Like a journal, recording your dreams to be studied later, can be beneficial for a myriad of reasons. As a calming activity to get your brain in gear for the day, recording your dreams can also help to give you perspective on your life. There may be a nugget of wisdom waiting to be mined in the deep recesses of what your mind has conjured for you in the night. Not to mention that, for creative people, dreams can often lead to new, innovative ideas for products, writings, or projects.

The best time to record your dreams is first thing in the morning. Immediately upon waking, the mind starts to forget the dreams it had spun for you during the night. So, the best thing to do is to write down every little element of the dream. Not only can this be a therapeutic activity to wake up to, but it can also help catch any small details you may miss if you wait. Some dreams slip right through our grasp the more we latch onto consciousness after a good night's rest, which will not help with the interpreting process. In order to properly interpret dreams, they must be recorded and even the smallest details can make all the difference. A snake slithering into a cottage in the woods is very different from a bunny hopping into the cottage. The whole context of a dream can change based on the most minute detail.

For some, a note-taking app works wonders for recording dreams. For others, however, a pen and notebook are ideal. If you are the easily distracted type, a phone may be too tempting with all its apps and social media badges to tap on. While a phone is faster, a pen and paper can help keep the vision in your head longer and help keep your brain focused on the images as they fade.

Chapter Three: What Do Your Dreams Mean?

The most enjoyable part about recording your dreams is interpreting them. More often than not, dreams have a way of showing symbols or patterns that signify things happening in our lives. These could act as little clues from the mind world, universe, or God(s) telling you which path you need to take next. The most important thing to remember is that the only expert on you is *you*. It is going to be vitally important to continuously ask yourself "what does this mean to me?"

To someone living in Cairo, a scorpion might mean something entirely different than it would to someone living in Alaska.

How To Interpret Dreams

Now the fun begins. To make it simple, here are some key steps to assist in your quest to discover what your inner self is trying to tell you.

Record your dreams. The most important part of interpretation is recording your dreams. As mentioned in the previous chapter, we forget key details the longer we are awake. Eventually, we forget the whole dream unless it is truly graphic and unforgettable.

Recognize emotions. Sometimes things happen in dreams that make us feel a certain way upon waking or have us feeling a certain way in the dream. Compare how you feel during the dream to how you feel after you wake up. Are the feelings the same? If they are different, ask yourself why. Incorporate the small details of your dream into the emotions and see if your feelings change.

Pinpoint common threads. Is there something popping up in your dream more and more often? This could be a place, person, item, or thought. If there is a common topic that you keep coming back to, maybe it is something that needs to be worked through during your waking hours.

Interpret small details. Now is the time to flip through the dictionary on the next pages and see which symbols are consistently appearing in your dreams. Make a list of these things, and see which ones occur most often. Are multiple signs and symbols appearing in your dreams? What might these signs be trying to tell you? This will be the most arduous and lengthy part of the process, but it is well worth it when you finally decipher what your dreams are telling you.

Interpret all your dreams. While we might be more inclined to interpret the most graphic or bizarre dreams, silly or boring dreams can give us more insight into your life. Sometimes, it is the tiniest, most insignificant things in our day-to-day existence that need the most modification. Dreams are often a pathway to a new perspective our waking selves cannot sense. Perhaps a dream about sitting in a classroom you have not seen in several years is a message to reach out to a high school friend. Or it could be a sign that going back to college may be meant for you. Do not discard dreams because they seem boring or mundane on the surface.

Symbols and Meanings

For many, dreams are not very straightforward and require a very attuned mind to get the right message from these coded images. The following is a compilation of common symbols that have generic meanings that you can apply to your dreams. However, these symbols are by no means concrete. For you, eggs may not signify fertility issues like they may to someone else. It is imperative that you use your intuition when interpreting. If the given meaning does not fit, try meditating on the symbols and write down the first few things that come to mind. Those answers are likely how you view the object or concept.

Abdomens. When you see your abdomen in a dream, it often is a reflection of the gut feelings you are having. The stressors you may feel deep inside could be driving you in a certain direction. Take into account your emotions when you see your abdomen in the dream.

Academies. Seeing an academy or university in a dream could be a signifier of two things: personal growth and academic growth. Perhaps you seek someone to help you develop your personality, skills, or emotional arsenal. It could also be representative of a desire to put some academic skills under your belt. Is there excitement or fear at seeing the academy? If you are afraid to pursue something even though you want it, this could be your dreams pushing you to embrace the fear and let it fuel your drive. If you have been thinking about returning to college and an institution of higher education appears to you, it may be time to enroll.

Acorns. Representing strength and development, acorns can be seen during especially challenging times. However, acorns are a good thing to see. Acorns normally mean you are meeting the difficulties of your life head-on and with the required fervor. Keep going. This too shall pass.

Airplanes. As with most vehicles, airplanes represent change. Airplanes are the fastest common mode of transportation in the human arsenal, so this is indicative of rapidly approaching change. Perhaps you feel the need to move in a different direction in life. Is your job too challenging or not challenging enough? Is there something that needs to be switched out? Excitement on a plane indicates a desire for change while fear and anxiety about takeoff could mean you do not feel you are ready for the changes to come.

Babies. While some people may get immediately uneasy at the appearance of a baby in their dreams, it certainly does not automatically indicate a coming pregnancy. although, it can if you are trying to have one or are thinking about having one. Sometimes babies represent our maternal or paternal side, our desire to nurture those around us, or the desire for a new beginning. It is always important to keep in mind the emotions you are having while in the dream, as well as what is happening with the baby. If the baby is being colicky or crying, it could be a reflection of your need for love and desire for attention. If you are the one caring for a baby in a dream, it could be signaling a desire to start over in an aspect of your life.

Blood. Sometimes the presence of blood in a dream can automatically make the dream feel like a nightmare, but it isn't always a bad thing. Blood inherently is indicative of our energy and lifeforce. When it is your blood being spilled, it could signal a need to retreat and take care of yourself; a spa day, a sleep-in day, or a sabbatical from work could be the inner desire being expressed. Sometimes the blood of others spilling could mean that we feel we are not getting enough energy from a person in a relationship.

Blood is also sometimes equated to greed. When the blood is spilled violently, this could be a discourse of a greed-driven action in your life that you may need to atone for; or if you are the one being hurt, this could be a sign to let go of the greedy action someone took that victimized you.

Buried Alive. Being buried alive automatically sounds like a nightmare, but there is likely more meaning in it. You can turn this nightmare into a silver lining, although we cannot change the experience of actually having to dream it. Being buried alive suggests struggling with too many obligations. Equated to drowning or suffocating, it is all about having too much on your plate and not enough time to finish anything up. You feel that you cannot catch your breath under the constant storm of needs. Is there too much required of you in your life? Perhaps it is time to cut back on some obligations until the feeling of overwhelm passes.

Beaches. The sea is often used to describe our subconscious mind, while the land represents our conscious mind. Because of this, the shore is where the two meet. Standing on the beach may be a sign to dive deeper into the unknown and learn more about the hidden gems of your own psyche. Let the waves of emotion and events wash over you as you grasp for bits of yourself hidden in your subconscious. Perhaps you feel like you do not know who you are or who you thought you were. Or this could be an indication to take a step back and relax as you try to figure everything out. Although a daunting practice, it is integral to finding more secure footing inside your psyche.

Clocks. Other than the obvious anxiety about the alarm clock in the morning or a lack of sleep, clocks represent all aspects of time interpretation. If you are with another person in your dream, this could be a manifestation of fear that you do not have as much time as you want with that person. A watch could be suggesting that you are searching for something in your life. Be mindful of what is happening to the watch, who is wearing it, or what the face says. Any of these aspects could change the context of the message.

Clowns. While many harbor a fear of clowns, the characters were initially created to bring happiness and fun. Usually, a clown appearing in your dreams is a recommendation to let go of fear and anxiety, as well as to try and laugh a little more. What is the clown doing? Where is it going? Perhaps the answers to these questions will give you context into which aspects of your life to ease up on.

Crashes. Everyone has experienced the same falling sensation while sleeping, but what about crashing? Sometimes, the crash in a dream is so intense that you jerk awake, panting, and looking around. This could signify that something in your life needs to stop immediately or that the need to stop is coming soon. This could be an addiction, or a toxic work environment. The stopping jerk may be a signal that you are being pulled back before impact, meaning this "stop" in your life will not crush you, but you may feel the whiplash. Be prepared for all aspects and consequences of the path you take in regard to this change in your life.

Crying. Not unlike twisting the cap off a bottle of soda left in a car all day, crying is about release. Think of yourself as the soda bottle, and the hissing it makes as your tears. When the pressure is released, the bottle is somewhat malleable and flexible. Are you holding anything inside, causing the pressure to start giving you emotional and physical discomfort? Consider the context of the dream: who you are with, what you are doing, and what are the emotions you are having? What emotions is your sleeping self trying to get your waking self to handle?

Deer. Almost always a good omen, deer represent blessings and fortune. These creatures are usually docile, and they tend to shy away from society. Focus on how the deer behaves in your dream. Does it come right up to you? Do you have to sneak up on it? This behavior should correlate to the way in which your blessings or fortunes come. Perhaps the fortune will drop into your lap, or you may have to be strategically placed in close proximity to your fortune.

Consider where the deer is located. If it is in a bizarre location for a deer, it could be a sign that your fortune or blessings will come from an unexpected place.

Demons. In dreams with demons, we are seeing ourselves. There may be an aspect of yourself that you are not content with that has manifested as the depiction of a demon. Take into account every little aspect of the world around you in this dream. Small things like a clock could mean that you have a big problem with time, a fear, anxiety, or stress that causes you to behave a certain way that you view worthy of expelling.

Diamonds. Social morays dictate diamonds mean commitment and a show of wealth. These are two possible meanings of diamonds in dreams. It also depends how you personally view diamonds. Someone who does not have a reverence for diamonds likely will not see one as a signal for commitment. Generally, receiving a diamond could mean you are ready for commitment while losing one could mean that this relationship is not ready to progress. Be mindful of who gives you the diamond, how the diamond is set (ring, necklace, etc.), and the location where the exchange of, or loss of, happens.

Dogs. While dogs can depict companionship and loyalty, they can also depict the most innate instincts within you. If you are the type of person longing for a companion or long-term relationship, a dog appearing in your dream may be trying to tell you to have patience, especially if it is a calm and watchful dog. A sniffing dog, as if searching out something, could be a sign that you are in need of something that you cannot seem to locate. This is more than likely an abstract idea (love, affection, or strength). If the dog is playful and enjoys playing with you, this dream could likely be about letting go of stressors and living in the moment, a subtle sign to stop letting little moments pass by unenjoyed.

Earthquakes. During an Earthquake, the very foundations of the Earth are shifting. Pressure is causing the crust to move in a potentially catastrophic way. The same goes for any emotions we bury deep inside. When the pressure of keeping those emotions and feelings buried becomes too much for you to bear, your foundation starts to change. This is symbolic of the need to release the pressure and right the foundation of your unconscious beliefs before the pressure knocks you off your feet.

Eggs. As mentioned earlier, eggs are a very common and ancient symbol of fertility. Many Goddesses use or are given eggs as part of their sacrificial altars. When an egg appears in your dreams, it does not always signify your chances of producing children. Sometimes, this fertility is a creative one. Are there any projects you have been thinking about doing? Are there any plunges you are ready to take but unsure if you should make the leap? It might be time to let them hatch and enjoy the fruit of your labors instead of sitting on the eggs in the nest, waiting.

Elevators. As a mode of transportation that goes up and down, an elevator has multiple meanings. Ascending upward could mean that you feel your progress toward mental or emotional health is progressing nicely. If the elevator is descending, it may indicate the opposite and it just may be time to re-evaluate how you deal with your mental and emotional development.

It is also important to note what is happening in the elevator. Are you pressing the buttons and not moving? Maybe you need to ask yourself what is preventing you from starting your movement to get to the proverbial floor you wish to access.

If the elevator crashes or comes to a sudden stop, a problem may be occurring in another area of your emotional health that must be worked on before the elevator can pass that particular floor.

Embarrassment. We have dreams where we are in a really awkward environment or situation. The common dream about being naked in public, having the door opened on you while using the bathroom, or farting during a presentation know no boundaries. A lot of the time, these dreams are more an explanation of our deepest insecurities, not our opposition to things we are actually afraid of. Being naked in public could be more about being surrounded by people and bringing your inner personality out, causing it to be exposed to people you may find undeserving of knowing your true self. This feeling makes you "naked" before them.

Consider what parts of you are being "exposed" in these embarrassing dreams and how they correlate to what aspects of yourself are being shown to others.

Faces/Facelessness. One of the most common themes in dreams is that of seeing a face or seeing a loved one, or oneself, as faceless. When we see a face in our dreams, it is indicative of knowing a person's identity or personality. If you are doing a skincare routine in your dream, smiling at yourself, or grooming yourself, it is likely a representation of how you feel about your progress in your personal growth and development. Fumbling with your skincare products may represent that you are not confident in your progress. Similarly, dreaming about someone else grooming themselves or you, for that matter, is indicative of their progress on their development or their hand in your development.

When we see our loved ones without a face it is almost always indicative of a lack of understanding about that person. If a loved one or even yourself is faceless, you are struggling with understanding that person or yourself. A lack of identity or personality could be indicated. Perhaps some quality time with the faceless person is in order. Or it might be time to look within if you are the faceless person.

Falling. No list of dream themes would be complete without the all-too-common occurrence of falling. Representing a need for stability, falling is among the most worrisome aspects of dreaming. If you jerk awake from the falling, you could be in desperate need for stability. When you are stumbling, your feet need the security of solid ground beneath them. As you fall, your feet are not on the ground. This could be indicative of how you are feeling about yourself. Do you feel like you have control of your life and your mind?

Fire. In ancient cultures, fire is viewed as a purifying element. Seeing fire in your dreams could signify your need to purify something in your life. The need to fix, renew, or find a passion for something could be indicated by the presence of fire. Something to consider is your feelings on the fire and what is burning. Is a photo being burned? The person in the photo could be removed from your life and thus leaving you a feeling of purification in their absence. Is a relic from your childhood being burned? This could be a representation of you being reborn with a new spark or passion in life.

What the fire is burning is an important contextual clue as to what is being signified. A campfire could indicate a sense of peace, while a house fire might be indicative of emotional distress.

Almost always, a fire is a positive sign as it indicates a motivation, drive, or the rekindling of passion.

Fish. Since fish live in the water, they are associated with the deep unconscious parts of us that we are not even aware of. The exoticness and strangeness of a fish is the measure of its representation in our subconscious. An Angler fish or Colossal Squid could be indicating something about our deepest unconscious that we were not aware of. Be vigilant about what the fish is doing. If the fish is speaking, walking on legs, or breathing air, your subconscious may be trying to tell you that you are capable of things your waking self may consider impossible.

As well as being representative of our deepest selves, fish are integral parts to almost every culture in ancient history. Fish signify abundance, joy, and blessings. Are you capturing a lot of fish in a net? Are you on a deep-sea fishing rig? Both of these may suggest that you feel you are gaining a lot of physical or emotional resources. Perhaps your life is full of blessings your conscious self cannot see.

Galaxies. Seeing galaxies is in a similar vein as seeing space. This can indicate the need for space, a need for a slow rebirth, or the desire to travel large distances. It is important to take into account what else is happening in the dream. Are you happy, scared, or anxious? These feelings could represent emotions in relation to the unknowns in your life. If you are with another person and feel negative, seeing a galaxy around them could mean you need space from each other or need to start over.

Garden. A retreat or a paradise for the person dreaming, a garden is typically the physical manifestation of your ideal safe space. The foliage of the garden represents growth and development, as plants are continually growing. If the plants in your garden are withered or sick, this could be an indication that you need to give more time and attention to your emotional needs.

Also note which animals are present in the garden. A snake, spider, or dragon could mean a danger or a threat to your emotional health within yourself.

Ghosts. The primary goal of ghosts is to haunt something or someone. That being said, seeing a ghost in a dream means that there is something or someone that is causing us to obsess. Sometimes this means that this subject is on our mind all the time, while other times it means this subject is driving our decisions. Take note of who the ghost is, if they are identifiable. This could point you in the direction of who exactly is making your mind feel so stressed.

Also take into account your history. Do you think you have some past trauma, blocked out memories, or hidden anxieties to work on? Sometimes our subconscious knows that there is something wrong, but our conscious selves are not aware of any issue. Small details help in narrowing this down: location, people around you, time of day, or actions of all parties involved. Is the ghost breaking things, touching you, or simply standing still? If the ghost is being destructive, it could mean that the root of the issue is damaging to you. If they are standing still, they may be making you feel uneasy and need to be let go.

Gods/Goddesses. Gods or Goddesses sometimes appear in our dreams, whether they are from ancient cultures, biblical times, or are unnamed. Because Gods are often viewed as perfection and the embodiment of a higher existence than that of humankind, this may be an example of something you feel about yourself or desire to feel about yourself. Note what the God or Goddess is doing. If they are doing something kind or positive, this could be a reflection of one of your most elite traits. If the God or Goddess is corrupt and taking pleasure in something negative, you may be feeling that you embody negative traits.

Goddesses, in particular, represent feminine energy, which can also extend to nurturing, kind, or mature traits. If you are feeling positive and happy to see this Goddess, you may feel worthy to be in her presence because you embody these kind attributes. If you are scared, anxious, or negative you may feel unworthy and that you do not possess these attributes.

Another aspect to consider is if the God or Goddess reaches out to you, are they inviting you to be one with them? This could be your subconscious telling you that you possess more positive traits than you think, and you must embrace yourself more.

Hail. Water, specifically rain or crying, represents a release of pent-up emotions. But what does it mean when the water is frozen? The hardening of this release into hail makes it so that the emotions cannot escape. Hail is a signifier of the threat that these emotions cause when they are not let go. Representing the pressure of difficult emotions and the inability to express these emotions, sometimes due to environment or lack of a trusted confidant, hail is indicative that something is wrong, and it needs to be corrected. Perhaps seek out a friend to help you talk out the issues popping up in your mind.

Consider who is in the hail. Is someone being hurt by the hail? Are you being hurt by the hail? If there is someone there with you? This may be an indication that this person could be collateral damage from the threat your emotions have on you. Perhaps this is a warning of an emotional meltdown that can be prevented with a good advisor or companion.

Hallways. A hallway has many doors. This could be your subconscious deciding which of your memories to access. It is also representative of gatherings, and much like a hotel, this could be signaling of different personalities molding together. Are you building aspects of yourself from other people? This is not a bad thing, but be aware of which parts you take from other people.

Take into account if the hallway is full or empty. If the hallway is empty, maybe a forgotten memory wishes to resurface, or you are feeling like you need to add something to your social life.

High Schools. All schools are generally representative of our previous selves. Who we were in our formative years are the building blocks for the adults we became. High schools, or schools of any kind, indicate a piece of ourselves we may feel is gone. Perhaps write down your waking ideas and thoughts when you think of high school. One of the aspects that is missing may be something you would like to revisit.

Note that a school is equivalent to your age. High schools in dreams means that your subconscious wants you to focus on the age range in which you attended that school.

Hourglasses. An hourglass is another representation of time. The grains of sand appear slower, which means that you are concerned something may be creeping up on you. Is there a due date approaching? Perhaps an ending of something that could be on the horizon is giving you undue stress? Take a good, long look at your calendar.

Ice. As water represents the release of pressure and emotions, ice often represents an obstruction. Like hail, ice can signify a need to melt away something keeping you feeling stuck. Consider where the ice is located. Are they in the form of icicles hanging from your bedroom windows? This could represent a danger coming due to pent-up emotions, an emotional breakdown, or lashing out.

If you are walking on the ice and cannot get your footing, this could be indicative of a perceived lack, or loss, of control.

Infidelity. At its root, infidelity is about dishonesty. Dreams including infidelity may not be about cheating or adulterous behavior. There could be something in your life that you feel has hints of dishonesty. Ask yourself if you are being dishonest with someone or if you feel someone is being dishonest with you.

Take note of who is being dishonest in the dream. If it is you, it might be time to come clean about something.

Injuries. In dreams, injuries are more indicative of what is happening on the inside. Injured people are usually a sign of emotional trauma. An injury on the chest could be suggestive of heartache or feeling heartbroken. An injury to the legs could mean a sense of feeling stuck or trapped. An injury in the arms may be something to do with having trouble letting go of something.

Islands. Usually associated with a pleasant experience, an island represents the need to enjoy the simple things in life while trying to let go of anxieties. You may see a vacation is in order.

However, remember to take into account the context of the dream. If there is a storm or you feel trapped on the island, perhaps you are not taking something seriously enough.

Jail. A jail is a restrictive thing. This is a representation of feeling stuck, trapped, or restricted. The presence of a Police Officer or Prison Guard may indicate that you feel trapped by someone; all the more insightful if the officer is someone you know.

Is there someone in the jail cell with you? Depending on who this person is may give you further insight into what makes you feel trapped.

Jewelry. When jewelry is involved, it is time to think of ancient civilizations. Often considered a symbol of good fortune, blessings, or opulence, jewelry in your dreams could indicate that you feel something good has come your way. On the other hand, if the jewelry is broken or being broken, this could indicate a feeling of loss, bad fortune, or poverty. Also note who the jewelry belongs to and who is wearing or breaking the jewelry.

Jungles. Like the ocean, a jungle represents the unknown in your unconscious mind. A little more dangerous than the ocean, the jungle is rife with creatures, is a vast expanse to get lost in, and has dense vegetation. This could be indicative of feeling like you have too many thoughts that make you feel overwhelmed and lost.

Objects you find in the jungle could give context to the things that make you feel overwhelmed in your own thoughts. Animals from the jungle could be potential Spirit Guides for those who believe in that sort of thing or, could indicate your fierceness level.

Juries. A jury passes judgement. Seeing a jury indicates the feeling that you are on trial and need to defend yourself for something. If there has been a recent event that you feel you are being scrutinized over, perhaps your mind is telling you to either let go or come clean. Has the jury been asked to pass a penalty on you? Are you on the jury and sentencing someone else? These are also important details to take into account. If you are passing judgment on another person, perhaps you feel they need to answer for something, or your subconscious could be indicating that you are too judgmental of others.

Keys. A symbol of exploration and discovery, keys indicate that there could be something hidden away that needs to be found. Important things to consider are: who is holding the key? what is it used for? Where is the location of the locked items?

If you are holding or using the key, this could mean you have discovered something about yourself or someone else. If someone else holds the key, they may be discovering something about you. The location of the locked item indicates who the information is about. Is it your childhood home? If so, the information could be a repressed memory. Is the locked item in a friend's house? Perhaps you feel they are hiding something from you.

Also consider the object or place that is revealed with the key.

Killing/Killed. Killing can be a good thing or a bad thing. Sometimes, we have to remove something from our lives and when we dream of that thing being killed, it is a reassurance from our subconscious that this is a good path for us. Take into account the thing being killed. Killing a snake can represent the removal of deceit from your life. Killing a spider, however, could represent a piece of your creativity being killed, which may or may not be a good thing for you.

If you are the one doing the killing, take into account how you are feeling about it. If you are experiencing negativity while doing the act, this may indicate that you should not be purging this thing from your life.

If someone else is killing something of yours, you may feel victimized by this person and that they are subduing parts of you.

King. A king is a strong man with characteristics of opulence, strength, and power. When you are expressed as a king in your dreams, you have the ultimate control. You may feel that you can handle any challenges that come. If you are looking at a kingly outfit, but not wearing it, your subconscious may be telling you that you are within reach of attaining these attributes, or that you have a deep desire for these attributes.

Ladybug. A ladybug represents good fortune and attractiveness. A ladybug landing on you is seen as good luck and thus seeing one in your dream may have a similar meaning. The color is also important. White ladybugs could be indicative of purity while red ladybugs could mean passion. This does not necessarily mean you will or will not have a partner. The purity or passion is in a metaphorical sense. Purity, in this case, means you may view yourself with a level of honesty, loyalty, and ethics. Passion could be in lines of a hobby, creativity, or something of deep importance worthy of your time.

Lemons. Lemons are a good omen. Indicating a lust for life, lemons may mean you have a passion for adventure, an excitement for exploration or travel, or a deep desire to experience everything in life. It also represents taking something negative and transforming it into a positive. If you are holding, eating, or drinking from a lemon, you may believe these are attributes you have. If you are picking lemons from a tree, you may be in the process of developing these characteristics.

Lions/Lionesses. There is a reason the lion is called the King of the Jungle. Animals in dreams could signify that the particular creature is your Spirit Guide. Think about what a lion represents. Often the model of justice, courage, respect, and wisdom, lions are held in a very high regard within dreams. Who do you feel the lion is representing? Is the lion watching, attacking, or hunting? The action the lion is taking could be indicative of how you view yourself or of an attribute you need to adopt.

If the lion is attacking something, this could be indicative of the need to protect. Is there something or someone in your life you feel the need to protect? Perhaps you are the person you feel needs protection.

Lionesses have an integral role in the pack. As the hunters and fierce nurturers of the group, Lionesses are the symbol of strength and power as well as motherhood. Hunting Lionesses could mean that you feel you need to provide something for someone. If a Lioness is bringing you something, perhaps there is something you need that you do not feel you have.

Lust. Dreaming of being overcome with lust can be fun, but it often signifies that you are missing something. Lust can mean there is an incompleteness that we may be feeling but we are not aware of what is missing. Also a sign of satiation, Lust can mean that you do not feel satisfied by something in life. Examples include your job, relationship, or hobbies.

Being possessed by a lustful emotion could also indicate a perceived lack of control in life. Do you feel you are driven by forces outside of your control or that you have little control in your most intimate aspects?

In a more straightforward context, intense Lust could be your subconscious telling you that you need to control yourself a little more and perhaps look inward for intimacy rather than outward.

Magic. A positive sign, Magic indicates exploration and discovering the hidden parts of our psyche. Magic is symbolic of malleability, change, and transformation. This can also mean personal development and growth, but is more relative to discovery of ourselves and our happiness. When in a dream, if we utilize an object to conduct the Magic (a wand, staff, or other object), the indication is that we are actively controlling the Magic. With this under our control, the discovery is all our own and we can change ourselves and all aspects of ourselves at will.

When the Magic is utilized by someone else in your dream, the indication is that you feel there is little control over the transformation.

Mansions. Similar to hallways, mansions have many rooms and functions. The many rooms indicate memories, experiences, or parts of the psyche that the conscious mind may not be aware of. When you enter a room in a dream mansion, it may indicate a repressed memory, an old memory, or a part of your ego or mind that has been long forgotten.

Associated with finances, the more elegant your mansion, the more wealth you may desire. Older-looking styles of mansions may indicate the past while newer-looking styles may indicate your present or future, as perceived by you.

Note how you feel walking into the home. Is there any nostalgia? Do you feel there is hope? These answers may help you narrow down whether the mansion indicates your past, present, or future.

Consider who is in your mansion. People within your mansion may hold more of your trust. People in rooms closer to the front door have less of your trust, while those closest to the center or closest to your bedroom have the most of your trust. People outside your mansion have none of your trust.

One more distinction is if the mansion is haunted. A haunting in a mansion could embody an obstacle in the way you view your life, stability, or financial security.

Meteors. When we think of meteors, sometimes we think of shooting stars, on which we wish. Indicative of wishes, the meaning of the dream boils down to what happens to the Meteor. Is the meteor blowing up in the atmosphere? This could mean that the wish may begin to come true but not in the way you wanted it to. If the Meteor lands on your property, this could be an entirely positive sign that your wishes could come true.

What if the Meteor lands on your home or on your car, causing a lot of damage? The meaning could be that you are anticipating a wish coming true, but it will come with its own struggles. Prepare yourself emotionally and physically to deal with the dust that gets kicked up from the wish's impact.

Mirrors. A Mirror reflects our image, and thus helps us see who we really are. Connecting us with our subconscious view of ourselves, Mirrors are a significant object to be noted in your dream journal. What is the reflection you see in the Mirror? Is it you or is it someone you wish to be?

If you are smiling at your reflection, this could indicate that you are happy with who you are and the work you have done on your growth. If you are smiling at a reflection that looks to be a future you, then you are happy with the steps you have taken so far. Negative feelings in these examples indicate that you are not happy with who you are or what steps you have taken.

Broken or shattered Mirrors are not good signs, often an indication that your subconscious is struggling with a disconnect between your true self and how you view yourself. Are there major flaws that have caused disturbances in your relationships? Investigate inward and list any negative traits that you would like to fix. Note what Mirrors look like in future dreams.

Nakedness. Being naked is a straightforward symbol meaning vulnerability and exposure. When you dream of people around you being naked, you may feel that you know them more than you ever have before. It could be a result of a deep conversation in which someone has confided in you or the feeling of closeness with someone.

Embarrassment often accompanies this feeling, but note if this emotion is within the dream or outside of it. Embarrassment with the nakedness in the dream may indicate that you feel awkward about the closeness you share with another person.

Nakedness could also be a symbol used by your subconscious to ask yourself to reevaluate how you view the aspects of yourself you dislike or how you hold yourself in social interactions.

Natural Disasters. Storms of any kind usually indicate emotional turbulence. The more intense and destructive the natural disaster, the more intense your subconscious might feel about what is happening in your life. While rain, flowing water, and rivers indicate a release of emotions, a natural disaster could indicate the destructive way in which your subconscious wants to release the emotions. Do you feel the desire to destroy things?

Take note of what things are being destroyed in your dreams. Is it your home? If so, this could indicate your subconscious has some turbulent feelings about your home environment or relationships with those in your home.

Nets. When a fish gets trapped in a net, it is seen as the beginning of the end for them. Nets represent feeling trapped, stuck, or captured. Nets belong in water, which indicates your unconscious or emotional release. Therefore, nets could be intimately linked with the feeling of being trapped specifically by your emotions or feelings buried inside.

A net on dry land may indicate that there is an issue you are already aware of that needs to be dealt with.

Is there an emotional trauma or life event that you have not gotten over? Note who is with you. Are you the fish being captured? Is the net on dry land or in the water? Is someone you know casting a net over you? The people appearing in your dream may indicate that your subconscious believes they have a hand in your stuck or trapped feelings.

Nurses. The role of a nurse is to nurture, which could be indicative of your subconscious asking for help. A dream in which you are taken care of by a nurse may mean that your subconscious believes there is a portion of you that must be healed. If you are becoming a nurse, then your subconscious may be trying to convey that you have all the tools you need to heal yourself or provide healing assistance to others.

What are you doing in the dream? Are you healing someone you know or perhaps looking in a mirror? If you are walking down a hospital corridor, your subconscious may be asking you to take the healing process slowly and solve one aspect of yourself at a time.

Oasis. An Oasis is a symbol of hope, salvation, and refreshment. Usually located in a desert, an Oasis is often the thing that someone traveling through the sand clings to in order to survive. An oasis in your dream may be your subconscious asking you to hold onto something or someone as a lifeline to get through a difficult time.

Take note of items that may be littered around both the desert and oasis in the dream. You can determine what room or place the oasis represents based on the items in the oasis. If your bed is in the oasis, then your bedroom may be a safe place for you to explore yourself. If there are people in your desert, then your subconscious may view these people as contributors to your negative feelings. These feelings, indicated by desert or sand, could include solitude, shame, or embarrassment.

Oceans. Like all forms of water, the ocean connects with the emotional subconscious while you dream. While crying means a release of emotion, oceans are more about the collective of what we do not know lingering in our subconscious. Anything seen below the surface can be indicative of aspects in your subconscious. Think about what you are seeing.

Are you scuba diving, snorkeling, or swimming in an Ocean? This could mean that you feel you are currently in the process of exploring your subconscious. Take into account whether you are happy with what you find.

Are you on a boat, skating over the surface of the water? This could indicate that you subconsciously believe that you are not searching through yourself very deeply, opting to only look in rather than swim (or sort through it with a hands-on approach). Those in therapy for mental health, for example, may see themselves swimming in the ocean more than those who are not in therapy.

Are there people under the surface of the water? Anyone in the water could be important figures in your subconscious, your view of the world, or how you view yourself. Objects could be floating in the ocean as well. Shipwrecks, underwater ships, or ghost ships could be your subconscious' view of a relationship that did not end well or has a rift.

Also important to note, is the color of the ocean. The darker the water, the less you know who you are. If you are swimming through a crystal blue ocean, happily enjoying the waves, you just may have figured out exactly who you are.

Oranges. Associated with many things, including wealth, success, and creativity, Oranges are closely representative of the sacral chakra, the second of the seven chakras, located just above the naval. Seeing an Orange in your dreams could indicate satisfaction and happiness, unless, of course, you are reaching for it, and it disappears.

What is happening with the oranges? Are they accompanied by other fruit? Are you holding, eating, selling, or squishing an orange? Holding and eating an orange could be indicative of your own happiness and satisfaction. Selling oranges could mean that you feel you know how to make other people happy, or you have something to offer someone to make them happy. Squishing or destroying an orange could mean that you are sabotaging your own happiness and getting in your own way.

Be mindful of who else is in the dream, if there are Mirrors involved, or if other people are eating the oranges as well.

Owls. At the forefront, owls suggest wisdom and intelligence. Often seen as one of the many Spirit Guides in the Magical realm, Owls are known for their cunning and prowess. Dreaming of an owl could mean that your subconscious feels you embody these traits. Among an Owl's other meanings are insightfulness and the darker parts of the psyche. Because Owls are nocturnal creatures, they often represent what the subconscious believes that you must see.

Take note of what the Owl is doing. Is the Owl meant to be you or someone you know?

Parades. A Parade is often the subconscious symbol of a distraction. This is the subconscious warning you that something is pulling you away from the goals and aspirations you have set in life. Sometimes born out of fear, a Parade is indicative that you need to refocus on what you truly desire.

Make note of the people in your Parade. These people may be those that your subconscious feels are leading you away from what truly matters to you. The people most front and center are likely the people with whom your subconscious holds the most qualms with. If you are front and center, this is your dream telling you that you are getting in your own way, that you are lost, or that you have no aspirations at the current moment.

Make note of the colors in the Parade. Dark Parades can have dark themes, like death, loss, and mourning. When a darker Parade is present in your dreams, this could be your subconscious signaling that there are people and items in your life distracting you from mourning or getting over some kind of loss. Heartbreak could be indicated by your subconscious if heartbreak symbols are present. Shattered hearts, dirty wedding bands, or shattered picture frames could be possible signs. Heartbreak symbols are very particular to each person or relationship, so be advised of your own by writing down which physical objects or actions come to mind when thinking about it.

A colorful Parade could indicate that something shiny or new is distracting you from your true aspirations. Because the colors are present, there is a distinct lack of pain, loss, or discomfort. Instead, there is light, happiness, and color. These could be the subconscious feeling overwhelmed with it all and warning you to seek back the stability of your aspirations.

Carefully note where the Parade ends. What is the location and what does this location mean to you? Is it a large, bustling city or is it a childhood home? The former could mean that the distraction itself can be a steppingstone in your success while the latter may indicate the subconscious need to let go of the past in order to move on.

Pearls. You are considered incredibly lucky to find a Pearl in the wild. Because of this, Pearls indicate both wealth and luck, and, by extension, success. A sign of affluence, even in dreams, Pearls can be the subconscious symbol of calm, peace, and generosity. The meaning, however, can change depending on the context. A Pearl necklace can mean loyalty and it should be carefully considered who is wearing the necklace and what that person means to you.

One other meaning behind the Pearl could be to protect children. Consider if there are children present in your dream, if you are the child, or giving a pearl to a child. This can change the context of the dream to show whether you are nurturing someone or if someone is nurturing you. Perhaps your subconscious wants to make you aware of someone doing more for you than you think.

Pets. The primary meanings of Pets are unconditional love and loyalty. Also, they could be the subconscious way of indicating instincts and primal desires, but those are less common. Usually, Pets are the dream's way of saying that something or someone has an aspect of love and loyalty for you. People in your life could present as a Pet. Even you, the dreamer, could be represented as a Pet.

Consider what is happening in the dream and who is the Pet. Are the Pet or Pets leading you somewhere? If so, what location do you end up in? These are important questions to answer as they will give more context to the dream. Being led through a foggy forest could indicate the subconscious being confused in your direction in life, while being directed through childhood streets could indicate a need to let go of the past.

Study your feelings on Spirit Guides. The most common Pets are cats and dogs, which are very prominent Spirit Guides. This may be the subconscious calling for you to adopt certain qualities of the Pet leading you.

Pianos. The Piano is the foremost of the sophisticated musical instruments. Tied to classic artists like Debussy and Mozart, the Piano is a significant sign for the subconscious. A representative of the subconscious, creativity, control, and mastery, the Piano usually appears when we feel we need more control over our lives, or we feel we embody control and mastery. This largely depends on who is playing the Piano and what we are doing in the dream.

Are you studying the Piano and being mentored? Then you may feel you are learning to take the reins of your life and the person teaching is showing you how.

Is there a large audience watching you perform? The subconscious could be nervous about the number of eyes on you and your actions. A mistake on the keys while in front of a crowd could indicate a lack of confidence. If you are alone while playing, then you may have more focus and attention on yourself, choosing to block out other's opinions and insertions into your life.

Because the Piano Keys are "keys", these could indicate unlocking something, starting over, or being reborn as well. Make note of how you view the keys and how your fingers look playing them. If something looks off, you may want to consider whether you feel you are faking some emotion or living an authentic life.

Quarrels. Rather obviously, a Quarrel in a dream may indicate the subconscious feels negatively about someone in your life, the person you may be quarreling with. However, this can be more indicative of you struggling with yourself and your own expression.

Queens. A Queen is regal and powerful. A dream including a Queen usually indicates a subconscious influence. Are you the Queen? Perhaps you have a natural ability for diplomacy that your subconscious is trying to laud you for. This would also include the ability to use information wisely. When viewing yourself as a Queen, your dreaming self may be telling you that you can be trusted to keep secrets, guide others in a good direction, and lead.

If another person is the Queen in your dream, your subconscious may be trying to signal that you need to embody more of the regal and powerful attributes of a Queen. If you see a Queen in the reflection of a mirror, this could mean that you desire to have more power and authority. Happiness shown within that reflection may mean that you are on your way to getting these attributes.

The Queen in your dream may also be someone you deeply admire. Take note of who it is and list the attributes of this person that you would like to embody.

Quicksand. Sand of any kind is usually a negative sign in dreams. Quicksand, as its name indicates, may be a sign of a sharp stagnation or halt in progress. If you are sinking in the Quicksand, your subconscious may feel that you are being sucked back into a past struggle, stumbling over something, or having a hard time letting go of something.

Is there someone around with a rope? Is someone attempting to save you? If another person is trying to save you, your subconscious may be trying to tell you that you can trust this person to help you get out.

Are you holding the rope and intent on saving yourself? This could be your subconscious telling you that you can handle the situation on your own.

Take note of the environment as well. If the Quicksand is in the middle of a city, this could indicate that the struggle or obstacle halting your progress may come from an unexpected place. If the environment seems appropriate for the Quicksand, then your subconscious may be trying to tell you to keep your eyes open in problem areas in your life.

Quarantines. A new favorite word after 2020, Quarantines may have taken on a new dream context for many people. The most common meaning of a Quarantine in a dream is isolation, emotional or otherwise. Sometimes this isolation is not a good thing but sometimes it is. The only way to know for certain is to see which other elements appear in your dream. Are you Quarantining away from a specific person? Is there someone banging at your door and trying to get inside? This may be your subconscious warning you away from that person because they are a perceived threat.

Another potential meaning of a Quarantine could be cutting a person or habit out of your life. Take note of whether you are on your phone, speaking to people. If so, the Quarantine is likely about a habit or addiction.

A third possible meaning is if you are not the person in Quarantine, but someone else is. This may be your subconscious wanting you to reach out to this person because of a perceived issue they are having - potentially an emotional trauma.

After recent Quarantines around the world, Quarantines in a dream could also be a subconscious fear of being trapped, isolated, or alone. Take note of how you are feeling during this Quarantine. Happiness and indulgence in hobbies may indicate a subconscious need for space and time in order to rejuvenate. Negative emotions such as anxiety, nervousness, or fear could indicate that your subconscious does not want to be alone and requires the aid of a support system.

Rafts. Like boats, canoes, kayaks, or any seafaring object, rafts indicate how you handle your emotions (as the emotions and subconscious are represented by the ocean, sea, or lakes). The important things to note in dreams with rafts are the conditions of the water and its depth.

Is the water dark and murky? This would indicate that the subconscious is dealing with a lot lurking under the surface and better equipment may be required to explore these waters (the equipment could be likened to therapy, medications, or the help of other professionals). Clear waters could be a reassurance by your subconscious that it knows exactly what emotions you are struggling with.

Is the water calm or turbulent? If you are dealing with rapids, a tidal wave, or a waterfall, your subconscious may be warning of some very intense emotions. If the water is calm, there may be a lingering emotional trauma, but the intensity of it is low. Perhaps this can be easily solved, and your subconscious is urging you to take care of this emotion before it becomes the aforementioned tidal wave.

Ravens. The subject of much scrutiny and poetry, the Raven is a very intelligent and clever bird, if a bit *ravenous*. Representing the subconscious' appetite for information, the presence of Ravens could be your dreaming mind telling your awake mind that you need to learn more about a topic. The number of Ravens could be the measure by which your subconscious wants something.

Ravens have bad qualities as well. Notorious for their destructive nature, dreaming about Ravens could be your subconscious mind warning you that in order to attain your goals, you must be willing to get your hands dirty, whatever that means to you. It's time to refer to your ethical code. What are you willing to compromise about yourself and your morals in order to get what you want?

Take note of what the Raven(s) are doing. Eating may indicate that you have to destroy something to get what you want. Flying may indicate the need for perspective (to see the broader picture, for example). Gathering in Flocks may be the subconscious desire to find like-minded people to help attain your goals.

Reindeer. A positive sign, the Reindeer is known for guidance. Particularly pertaining to social situations, friendships, or gatherings, Reindeers indicate that your subconscious may desire a change in your circle of friends. Not that these friends are bad, but because there may be more perspectives, friendships, or relationships that could offer you more positivity in your life.

Another aspect of a Reindeer is listening and watching. Your subconscious may be warning you to do these activities more. Are you more of a talker or listener when a friend is telling a story? If you find yourself interrupting a lot, speaking over people, or talking more than listening, a Reindeer could be your subconscious telling you to listen more intentionally.

Reptiles. Reptiles are known for requiring very specific living conditions due to their cold-blooded nature. Because they are cold-blooded, your dreams may be indicating that someone in your life is being cold to you or perhaps you are being cold to someone else. Your subconscious could be asking you to be aware of the people around you and the effect they have on your energy levels and emotional health.

A good sign about Reptiles in dreams is that they can represent thick skin, meaning you do not let things get to you too much.

Safes. The function of a Safe is to keep things secure. This could be your subconscious asking you which things truly matter to you, which things you need to keep close. This could also be a warning about locking yourself away emotionally.

Carefully notice which things are inside the safe. Are there family heirlooms, money, or pictures? The meaning of the Safe can change depending on the items stored inside. These could represent emotions, feelings, memories, or physical possessions.

One important distinction is if the Safe is broken and who has broken it. Your subconscious may be expressing emotional tension from a perceived betrayal from the person who breaks your Safe.

Salt. Meaning protection, healing, good luck, and preservation, Salt could be a subconscious way of showing that your negative emotions are being turned into positive emotions. Similar to finding a silver lining in negative situations, the presence of Salt could be your subconscious' way of reassuring you that things will be okay.

Observe what is happening with the Salt, as well. If you are making a line or circle, this could be your mind discussing the need for boundaries with someone or something. Be aware of the environment, the people, or the things in the area where you are making the salt line or circle.

Schools. The ultimate symbol of the past, Schools can indicate unresolved trauma from childhood, missed opportunities, or innocence. Sometimes, a School could also be your subconscious' way of accessing old, repressed, or forgotten memories to keep them alive.

The most important factor when it comes to a School in dreams is what is happening. Are you going to class? This could indicate a desire to go back to easier times. Are you walking through the empty halls? This may be your subconscious using old memories or discussing a potential feeling of loneliness.

If you are a teacher in a school full of children, you may feel like you have a lot to teach a younger person in your life. Being a teacher in an empty school could be the desire to share your knowledge with someone, but having no mentee to educate.

Selling. Sometimes when we are Selling something in our dreams, it's our subconscious trying to make us aware of how we perceive ourselves. If we are Selling something, we could be trying to make other people see what we have to offer and trying to prove that we are worth something. If someone else is selling something, perhaps your subconscious believes that they have a lot of personality to offer you. Take into account what is being sold. Is the item being sold meaningful to you? A house, an heirloom, or something you recognize as yours could change the context of the whole dream.

Tarantulas. Spiders, in general, represent feminine energy and creativity. Sometimes, however, they represent the dark and unknown side of our psyche. When a Tarantula is present in a dream, there is a discussion being had by your subconscious about your creativity, intuition, or emotional energy. Is the Tarantula attacking you or is it at peace with you? This indicates your current subconscious state with these aspects of your life.

Tattoos. A Tattoo is pretty much forever, meaning a Tattoo in your dream is something that has left a permanent mark on you. What is the Tattoo of? Make note in your dream journal what the Tattooed symbol means to you. Make note of where the Tattoo is. Is it close to your heart? Is the Tattoo visible to everyone in your everyday clothes? These questions indicate how important the situation represented by the Tattoo is to you, and if other people know about the situation.

Telephones. Telephone dreams are all about communication. If the line is broken, crackly, or generally uncooperative, this could be a sign from your subconscious mind that your communication with the person on the other end is troubled. It is probably a good time to discuss your relationship with this person.

Tombs. Things in Tombs could be considered buried or dead. Dreaming of a Tomb may be your subconscious bringing life back to an issue you had previously thought gone, put away, or resolved. Other times, Tombs can be the subconscious discussing hidden things. Old memories, hidden connections between major life events, or buried emotions could be the thing your subconscious is bringing to mind. Consider all the other events of the dream. The location, objects in the

Tomb, or names on the Tombstones are all important key details to take into account.

UFOs. The ultimate symbol of the out-of-this-world, the unknown, or the scary, UFOs usually symbolize your subconscious dealing with something completely out of the ordinary. If you are seeing a UFO, you might be feeling stagnant in your life and yearning to get your feet off the ground on a project. If you are an alien in a UFO, you might be feeling like an outsider in some situation. Consider what objects and places are in the dream and what situations your subconscious may be referring to.

Umbrellas. Because rain is a representation of emotion, or of getting emotions out, an Umbrella is the protection of yourself from other people's emotions. Take into account who else is in your dream. Is there someone causing the rain? This is your subconscious warning you to stay away from getting involved in someone else's emotional trouble. Alternatively, if you are offering an Umbrella to someone, your subconscious may be telling you that you can help someone else find their sunshine.

Unicorns. As a mythical creature, a Unicorn is a symbol of hope, mystics, and high standards. This is the embodiment of reaching for the stars and refusing to settle for anything less. This could be your subconscious giving you reassurance that your future is looking good, and that good fortune is going to come your way. Consider other objects in your dream as they could change the context of the dream. Are you riding the Unicorn? Is the Unicorn kicking you off? Have you only been able to give the Unicorn one single pat before it flies away?

The closer you are to the Unicorn, the more your subconscious is reassuring you. However, you are the best judge of how close is close enough.

Uniforms. Oftentimes, a Uniform is associated with a feeling of isolation. This could be your subconscious letting you know that you would benefit from being involved in a group of some kind. Or it could be your subconscious trying to warn you about losing your individuality. Take into account the context of the dream. Are you sticking out somehow, with no Uniform or with an odd-looking Uniform? This likely signals the former meaning. If your Uniform looks exactly like the others and you are unhappy in the dream, the latter may be what your subconscious mind wants your attention on.

Vampires. Usually a negative omen, Vampires in a dream indicate that someone around you may be sucking the energy out of you. Take note of what you are doing with the Vampire. Are you walking up and offering your blood to them? This could be your subconscious telling you that you are a willing participant in the emotional draining that another person does to you.

If you are a Vampire Slayer or killing a Vampire somehow, this is a positive sign. Your subconscious is telling you, in this case, that you are doing a good job purging your life of negative people and bad habits.

Vegetables. The ultimate sign of revitalization, Vegetables are often present in dreams when the dreamer feels that they need to refresh their mind and body. Also associated with growth and longevity, Vegetables are a positive sign. Consider which Vegetables are in your dream. A feast of Vegetables may indicate that your subconscious either feels you need more revitalization or that you have an abundance of it right now.

Vines. Some of the most determined plants in the known world, Vines are positive symbols. Representing positivity and motivation, Vines indicate a strength and a need to reach the top. However, if they are on the ground or pinning you to the ground, they could be a negative sign meaning you feel stuck or stifled. Consider what is happening in the dream, the people in the dream, or the objects in the dream. If other objects are stuck in the Vines, this could mean that the subconscious is discussing a situation as opposed to a person.

Volcanoes. Eruptive and chaotic, Volcanoes are all about pressure. Most often due to emotional or mental pressure, volcanoes are the subconscious' way of indicating there is something boiling under the surface. This could be the manifestation of repressed or hidden memories, emotions kept hidden and away from other people, or emotions you may be hiding or denying from yourself. This could be a warning from your subconscious mind that you need to be careful and deal with the issues you may feel are building up.

Walking. Indicative of mostly the subconscious view of your life path and life movement, Walking is a universal sign. Be attentive to the weather, the location, and the emotions of the dream while you are Walking. Any obstacles or difficulty moving forward could be the subconscious mind seeing an issue with your movement in life. Consider if there is something holding you back from doing what you desire to do in your life.

Take note of whether you are walking alone, walking slow, or in a dark environment. All of these could indicate obstacles or feelings of isolation, delayed growth, or difficult emotions.

Weddings. Representing bonds and commitment, Weddings are often depicted in dreams when the subconscious wants to talk about these themes. Perhaps your subconscious is reassuring you that you are ready to make that commitment. Objects, feelings, and events in a dream can change the context of the dream. A rainstorm flooding a Wedding may be a bad omen with the subconscious warning that intense emotions may play out if you go through with the commitment.

Weddings in dreams may not be indicative of a relationship but can pop up when any type of commitment is weighing heavy in a dreamer's life.

Whales. Because the ocean or sea is considered the deep unconscious territory where unknown feelings and emotions live, whales are messengers that bring the unconscious to the surface. Glimpsing a Whale in a dream is a push from the subconscious to dive deeper into the thoughts and feelings hidden inside your mind.

Wings. As a symbol of freedom, Wings often make an appearance in dreams when we feel protected. In a state of safety, we can spread our Wings and fly, thus the appearance of Wings is directly related to contentment and feeling safe. Flying, which Wings are tools for, is associated with lucid dreaming, and thus Wings are as well.

X-Rays. An X-Ray is all about seeing through the exterior, or through the surface. Seeing an X-Ray in a dream could be indicative of a deception or betrayal that you must see through. Make note of who is getting the X-Ray, the facility where the X-Ray is being done, and what part of the body is being X-Rayed. These questions will help you determine if your subconscious mind is directing your conscious mind to a deception, betrayal, or hidden knowledge that needs attention.

Xylophones. Just as a Xylophone is an interesting instrument, it holds a level of innocence. As such, it is often associated as an instrument that grounds the dreamer to the earth. Dreaming of a Xylophone means you care about the environment and the earth. Unless, of course, you are destroying the instrument. Take care to note the context in which a Xylophone appears in your dreams.

X - The Letter. The letter X almost always represents something crossed out, found, or purged. When you see a letter X in your dreams, it can mean you have "found the spot" or you need to pull away from something. This symbol is something that needs extra care and attention to decipher.

Where is the X located? If it is on the ground, the X is likely a symbol marking a spot. If the X is located somewhere on the ground, try to identify where that location is. If it is a childhood home, a current home, or a public place, the X may hold a special significance in the form of a memory.

If the X is located on a picture, a person, or a garment, this may be more indicative of a relationship with someone. Perhaps this is your subconscious' way of making your conscious mind aware that a relationship is no longer good for you.

Yarn. This symbol is most often associated with elderly women sitting in a rocking chair. Thus, Yarn represents routine. When Yarn appears in your dreams, it can mean that you are bored of the monotony of what you call your life. It may be time to shake things up by doing something new or different.

However, if the Yarn is tangled up and knotted, this may indicate that your subconscious feels confused, blocked, or stifled. This could be a warning that the monotony may cause you emotional distress.

Yawning. While some would think that Yawning is more an indication of tiredness, it is actually a sign that the subconscious feels lazy. This may be your subconscious wanting you to experience something new. Maybe your subconscious needs to refill its pool of memories, and this is its way of pushing you to make new ones for it to use.

Remember to use your own preferences. Sometimes the dream can give you an idea of what to do, but mostly the purpose of dreaming about a Yawn is to stimulate your senses.

Yellow. Like the sun, the color Yellow is associated with bright and shiny emotions. Happiness, intelligence, and enlightenment are all potential themes of the color Yellow. When this color pops up a lot in a dream, it could be on anything or the color of anything, but each type of object may mean different things. On clothing, Yellow could be how you see yourself or how you view the world. On flowers, Yellow may indicate pure joy. To dream of spitting up something Yellow would indicate a sickness, emotional or otherwise.

A good rule of thumb is to take the color's meaning and the object's meaning and mix those two together to understand what your specific dream means.

Zippers. To dream of a Zipper could mean one of two things. The first is the uncovering of something. This could be associated with nakedness or coming clean about a lie. Take into account who is unzipping something in a dream. If you are the one unzipping something, a jacket, jeans, pillow cover, or even a backpack, it could mean you are hiding a deceit of some kind. If someone else is unzipping something, your subconscious may feel that they are hiding something from you and need to come clean.

The more known and fascinating meaning behind a Zipper is sexuality. Unzipping something in your dream could be your subconscious telling you to be more open about sexual encounters, try something new, or think about where you truly lay on the sexual spectrum. Zipping something up, however, indicates putting up emotional walls and blocking people off.

However, if the Zipper is damaged or there is an obstruction, your subconscious may be trying to indicate that there is an underlying issue with sexuality that you have not confronted yet.

Zebras. Because of the split colors of a Zebra, this animal signifies balance and spirituality. Dreaming of a Zebra could be the subconscious' way of saying your beliefs may be too restrictive on your life. Your unconscious self may want a little more freedom than the strict boundaries you lay for it. Also note what the Zebra is doing in the dream. If the Zebra is peacefully grazing, this indicates an obstacle posed by your beliefs and boundaries. If the Zebra is aggressive with you, this could be the unconscious warning you that the beliefs may harm you in some way.

Zombies. The halfway point between the living and the dead, a Zombie in a dream means the subconscious has a disconnect somewhere. It is a common joke to say you feel like a Zombie when you are really tired or drained. A Zombie in a dream could be the subconscious trying to make your conscious self, aware that something is draining your energy. Often, Zombies are associated with more negative concepts than common tiredness. Also having to do with greed and overconsumption, zombies can indicate mindlessness. Your subconscious may be wanting you to take a good look at your spending habits and how you view the world.

Zoos. To dream of a Zoo is similar to dreaming of a jungle, except under a little more control. This is the subconscious discussing your more primal urges. In the dreams, Zoos may appear wilder, which can indicate how the subconscious views your primal urges. Take into account which animals appear in your dream Zoo and their behavior. Peaceful animals in captivity may indicate that your primal urges are not too intense, while feral animals may be your subconscious warning of the ferocity of your primal urges.

Chapter Four: Recurring Dreams, Deja Vu, & Lucid Dreaming

Other than the normal dreams that we have at night, there are special cases. Recurring dreams, deja vu, and lucid dreaming all have their place in our nighttime adventures. However, the questions about them have always remained. What do they really mean?

Recurring Dreams

Dreams that happen frequently, and over a long period of time, can be considered a recurring dream. Most often these dreams have negative associations more than positive associations. Sometimes stemming from trauma, you could often relive a terrible experience in your dreams time and again. This is largely a signal from your subconscious that a situation has impacted you in a deep and psychologically significant way. Perhaps consider seeking mental health services for any recurring dreams that prevent good sleep hygiene or contain overtly traumatic undertones.

There are also recurring dreams that are very common and have fewer negative associations. These typically include dreams about falling, flying, going to school, being naked, and being chased.

Most times, recurring dreams are usually an indication given by the subconscious that you have a consistent frustration, unmet need, or area of struggle in your life. As with all dreams, it is important to record recurring dreams and take careful note of all objects, people, and symbols in order to correctly interpret it. Many times, recurring dreams begin to stop when you take care of the underlying issue.

Deja Vu

The feeling of *déjà vu* is even less studied and expanded upon than dreams are. *Déjà vu*, stemming from the French words meaning "already seen," is the feeling of familiarity that something has happened to you before, even though it may not have. Some experts believe *déjà vu* is based more on experience or memory, but there is a theory that states *déjà vu* is deeply connected with the dreaming experience. A study done in the 1990's indicated that *déjà vu* is more closely related to dreaming as opposed to other theories. Patients in the study indicated that when they had *déjà vu*, it was something they had dreamed as opposed to just a familiar feeling.

Some experts further expand by saying that *déjà vu* could be a coping mechanism of the mind to make sense of experiences and make them less scary, a potentially evolutionary trait. Other theories suggest that because the mind composes many dreams a night, one or two of them are bound to come back into focus when there is a trigger for remembering them. However, because there is so little data to work with, all we know is that *déjà vu* happens. Some people believe a *déjà vu* to be a premonition of the future, so it would not hurt to record these in your dream journal as well. Maybe you will find that a specific episode of *déjà vu* means something important to you.

Lucid Dreaming

Of the specialty dreams, lucid dreaming may be the most fascinating. Lucid Dreaming happens when you are totally aware that you are dreaming. Lucid Dreaming also comes with the ability to control your dreams, change the plot, exchange the people, or rearrange rooms at will. Lucid Dreaming usually occurs during REM sleep, which is the point in the sleep cycle where the brain is most active. Because these dreams are the most vivid and graphic, Lucid Dreaming is likely easier and more effortlessly remembered during this time.

The benefits of Lucid Dreaming are not totally known, but some lucid dreamers have reported lessened anxiety and less traumatic dreams. The negative, however, is that Lucid Dreaming consistently and at will is a difficult task to accomplish.

To Lucid Dream, you will need to stay in the REM stage of sleep as long as possible, which may be hard for those who struggle with sleep. Having good sleep hygiene habits, like staying off electronic devices an hour before bed, consistent exercise, and a good sleep schedule will help you trigger a Lucid Dream.

Sometimes, a Lucid Dream can be your subconscious telling you that you are in control of your life and your path. As always, record and interpret the dreams, being careful to write down which aspects of your dream you were able to change or manipulate. Noting which things you have precise control over may indicate which parts of your life you feel need the most intentional change.

Final Words

Dreams have been an integral part of human life since the dawn of man. Since the Ancient Babylonians first began recording their dreams on stone tablets, dream interpretation has come a long way. Now, more than ever before, we know the different meanings to a hundred different subjects and topics. Using contextual clues, careful consideration, and dream dictionaries, like this one, human beings are better able to understand the mysteries of their dreams.

Rooted in personal experience, dreams have the ability to make you ask what path you should take and which relationships to foster. Many of life's personal questions, struggles, and wonders lie within our own mind, and our subconscious is constantly using memories, objects, and colors to help us get the right idea.

By using this Dream Dictionary, you are closer than ever to understanding your subconscious mind and better able to get clues from your inner self. The journey of taking control of your subconscious and learning about yourself has just begun. Enjoy the ride.

www.ingramcontent.com/pod-product-compliance
Lightning Source LLC
LaVergne TN
LVHW021738060526
838200LV00052B/3348